REDEEMED
BOUGHT WITH A PRICE

Ashley C. Slocumb

Creative Touch Publishing LLC.

Creative Touch Publishing

P.O. Box 7482
Warner Robins, GA 31095
ctpublishing14@gmail.com
www.creativetouchpublishing.com

Printed and bound in the United States of America

Ashley C. Slocumb
Redeemed: Bought with A Price

International Standard Book Number
978-0-578-43852-8

TABLE OF CONTENTS

DEDICATION

To God: I present every gift you have placed in me back to you. This is your story. I dedicate this book to you, that you may get the glory.

To Kayci, Kenya, Kaden, and Kylie: You have been my motivation and the source of my determination to not be defeated by the trials of life. This one is for you. Whatever you desire to be, pursue it! You can do all things through Christ who strengthens you.

To Every Young Woman: Who may be hurting, broken, feeling alone, and as though you are a nobody. To those who may be thinking you're too damaged to be used or loved by God. This book is for you!

ACKNOWLEDGEMENTS

To God: Without you I am nothing. This book would not exist without you. Thank you for positioning the right people and resources to help make this happen.

To My Husband Kenneth: Thank you for showing me what love is. You love me through all my flaws and for that I am grateful. Thank you for giving of yourself so unselfishly. I am grateful that God trusted me with someone as special as you. Thank you for every sacrifice you have made. You have been so kind, patient, and long suffering. Thank you for the example you are to those around you. We are blessed to have you!

To My Dearest Mommy & Stepdad, Cheri & Don: I am who I am because of your unwavering faith. Thank you for introducing me to Christ and allowing your lifestyle to show me who He is. Thank you for praying for me when I could not pray for myself, and for never losing hope in me. I can now understand and appreciate the tough love you gave. Thank you for your support with the girls. Know that you have inspired me in many ways. Your courage is one that I truly admire.

To Dad & Mum, Charles and Karen: Thank you for always backing me financially and never losing hope in me. You saw potential in me when I could not see it in myself. Thank you for loving me regardless of everything I have ever done.

To My Mother & Stepdad, Angelia & Cliff: Without you I wouldn't be here. Thank you for having the courage to reconnect and develop a relationship with me. You mean so much to me and I appreciate everything you do.

To My Spiritual Parents, Apostle & Pastor Akins: I am grateful for you. Your lifestyle outside of church has continually reflected what you teach and preach. I am thankful for leaders I can trust! Thank you for every call you've answered, every text you've responded to, every question you have answered, and every prayer you have prayed on my behalf. Thank you for believing in me, pulling out the gifts in me, and pushing me to be great.

There are numerous people who have played amazing roles in my life. I thank God for each of you being in the right place at the right time and for your obedience in assisting me in various stages of my journey. I pray God's blessings over each of you.

INTRODUCTION

I was raised in a strict Christian family along with one other sister, Jessica. Our parents, Charles and Cheri, sheltered us. My dad was in the Airforce. He was about 5ft 9 inches and fit perfectly between skinny and fat. He always kept his hair low and his dark brown skin was noticeably marked with scars from injuries. Dad played all kinds of sports; he was very athletic. He was a deacon in the church, worked a full-time job, and was also a student. My dad was fun to be around and, when in the company of others, he was most likely making someone laugh. However, because of his strict rules, I thought he was mean and unfair.

Dad loved a clean house. Our duties consisted of regular household chores but also included cleaning ceiling fans, washing baseboards, and window sills. He would say, "the house should be spotless." I remember running into my dad's room one day and asking if I could play outside with the other children. He agreed as long as my chores were done. After inspection, he pointed out that my sock drawer was not closed all the way and that there were a few socks sticking out of the top of the drawer. He went on to explain that I was on punishment. Much to my dismay, I watched as the other children played outside my window. Although dad never advised how long punishments would be, they were usually long. He would often say things like, "I'll let you know, or if you ask me again, I'm adding another week." I imagine the punishments only lasted a week but, at times, it felt like years.

We'd often look to mom for an escape from punishment but she always agreed with what dad said. She was a perfect replica of the virtuous woman described in Proverbs 31. My mother was submissive, righteous, and she loved God. She was simply beautiful. Her warm, welcoming smile earned her the nickname "Smiley." Her deep brown skin had a natural radiance. She was short but she stood firm on her beliefs and was not one to be taken advantage of. Mom was really good with her hands. She could braid, sew, and crochet. In her spare time, I often found her playing crossword puzzles. Mom was sweet, easy to get along with, and very laid back; she seemed content in all things. Outside of church I had only seen her cry twice.

She had acid reflux but before she was diagnosed with it, we had no idea what was going on with her. As a child, I remember hearing her cry out in agony. One day, tears ran down her face as she stood at the top of the stairway grasping her chest exclaiming it was hard for her to breathe. I recall being fixated on her as I stood at the bottom of the stairs. I couldn't move because I was concerned and wanted to know what was wrong with her. Seeing mom in pain was unbearable. She was the peacemaker of our home and when she was uneasy, I had no peace.

Mom was the foundation of our church going lifestyle. She had been raised in the church and likewise, she raised us in the church. Jessica and I sang in the choir, participated in plays, and were both active on the dance team; whether we wanted to be or not. My parents' strict teachings stemmed from our religious background. Based on their strict beliefs, we were not allowed to wear pants, fingernail polish, make-up or listen to music that was not gospel music. My sister and I did it anyway.

I remember living on a military base in San Antonio, Texas. At the time, I was approximately ten or eleven years old and Jessica was eleven or twelve. Our parents allowed us to ride our bicycles around the base, however, we were instructed to stay on the sidewalks and we were not to go too far. My sister and I never obeyed our parents' instructions. We rode to the BX, which was a store specifically for military personnel, their family members, and others who had access to the base. Because we lived very close to the BX we went there frequently. A drive there took less than 7-8 minutes. We often used our allowances to purchase nail polishes and music we were forbidden to listen to.

The first secular music I purchased was a cassette tape by Brittany Spears. My sister purchased the album "Writing on the Wall" by Destiny's Child. We learned of popular artists because we'd watch channels that played a variety of Hip-Hop and R&B videos, such as BET and MTV, when we were left home alone. We both liked Brittany Spears but we loved Destiny's Child. It was during that time that I fell in love with Beyoncé. I wanted to be just like her. I wanted my hair like hers. I wanted to move my body the way she did. I wanted the attention and I the popularity she had.

Without our parents' knowledge, my sister and I created a girl dance group. The group consisted of girls from the summer camp we attended. There we'd perform for the entire camp. Jessica was beautiful and an amazing dancer. She too was short and had a smile that could light up a room. Her skin was smooth and flawless. Her thick plump legs seemed to have been made perfectly for dancing. She had a personality that matched her outer appearance. . . in my eyes she was perfect. I recall being jealous of her when we were children because she was always entered into beauty pageants. When she was crowned as a winner, I'd secretly wish I was her.

I was tall, bony, and looked very different from my mom and sister. My skin bruised easily so I was covered in scars from bumps I'd picked at. I was also athletic like my dad, which is why he and I connected so well. We both loved sports. I was really good at basketball. Dad coached all of our recreational basketball teams. He was a great coach and I was a great player; I can count the number of times our team lost on one hand. I was much better at basketball than my sister Jessica, and I knew my basketball skills and performance made dad proud.

My mom and sister had more things in common and shared similar interest so they were closer. Similarly, dad and I loved sports so we were closer. I was considered a "daddy's girl" and Jessica was a "momma's girl." From the outside looking in people thought we were the perfect Christian family until my parents divorced.

CHAPTER 1
Divorce Before Marriage

My parents' divorce was a shock to our close friends and family members. There were no signs of trouble. Most people assumed their marriage was perfect because we were what appeared to be the "model family."

While going through the divorce my parents began the process of moving the family. By then, my dad had completed his military commitment at the base he was stationed at so it was time for him to transfer out to a new location in Georgia. Although both my parents prepared to move to the same state, they decided they would not reside together. My dad got an apartment and my mom found a house for us to live in.

Prior to moving to Georgia my sister and I lived in housing which was located on the military base. Life on base was different than living off the base. In order enter onto the grounds, it was required that one have a special ID which granted them admittance; it was considered to be much safer than living off of the base.

The housing complexes had playgrounds where children often gathered. Some rode bicycles while others skated. There were no gangs or reports of crimes.

Moving to Georgia was a culture shock. On Jessica's first day of high school she cried. Her new school was much larger than the one she'd previously attended. Public school also differed from the school we attended on base. Students were allowed to dress more freely in public schools. Young girls wore make-up and clothes so tight they looked as if they were drawn on. Because of our strict upbringing, my sister and I did not wear pants until third grade. Our mother never allowed us to dress as other children at the new school did.

My sister was scared and because she was scared, I became scared but did not show it. I didn't want my sister and mother to know that, at times, I was scared too. Without dad around I felt as though I needed to be tough for both my mom and my sister. Because I often hid my true emotions I was viewed as tough; sometimes nonchalant. Others who depended on me for strength had a shoulder to lean on but there were times when I needed someone too. Every so often I wanted my dad. There were many times when I hurt on the inside. . . I longed for him. I bottled those feelings and shared them with no one. I learned to hide the pain I felt and became someone else because I didn't want to be the little girl who was hurting. I didn't want to be the little girl who appeared weak.

I was very different from other children, especially those at the new school. While some embraced my differences, others mocked and laughed at me. I didn't like being bullied or picked on so I adapted quickly. I was quiet and conservative because of my upbringing but the children around me didn't like that and I didn't like being different.

I compared myself to others and I didn't like what I saw; I didn't like not fitting in with the popular group so I added to the new person I had become. Not only was I tough, I didn't allow others to bully me. I bullied them. I didn't want to be picked on or laughed at so I became the class clown. I felt better when others were laughing with me and not at me. I felt better knowing I was intentionally causing them to laugh.

Things were very different for my sister; she was popular and beautiful. Everyone loved and embraced her at the new school. Jessica was smart and she was a good student. She was a cheerleader and a member of a dance team outside of school. She was given moms' old car once she bought a new one. Although Jessica had numerous friends and appeared to be happy, I am sure there were things she also dealt with internally. The divorce was hard for both of us.

Without dad, I felt I as though I didn't have anyone. We were so close. I didn't understand how we had gone from talking every day to not speaking for days at a time, and sometimes even weeks, I felt as though he had rejected me. Dads' presence provided security. I looked to him for reassurance in everything so without him I had no direction. I didn't care what was happening around me because Dad was always there and he made me feel as if everything would be okay. I never worried while he was present because he took care of us. It was his motivation and his words that fueled me to play so well when I was younger; he pushed me in sports.

The new school I attended had a basketball team. I tried out and made it but I did not play to the very best of my ability. My surroundings were new and I didn't have my dad there to push me. I believe there were two underlying reasons why I did not play so well during that time. First was the fear of rejection. The second was that my passion for basketball left when dad left.

As I reflect back, I can see how the devil used divorce to introduce the spirit of rejection into my life. I felt that I had to protect both my mother and sister. In our new environment, I was not accepted by those around me, and because of the divorce I felt as though my dad rejected me as well. Both those situations led me to believe I had to become someone else. Those circumstances caused me to look at myself differently and feel I was neither good nor strong enough. I felt unworthy and that I needed to become someone else. Fear of rejection became a reoccurring issue in my life and lead to serious identity issues which paralleled to the need to have approval from others.

The fruit of my condition began to manifest in my new environment. I began getting in trouble and was eventually sent to an alternative school for children with behavior issues. An alternative school is specifically for children who have been expelled from their original assigned schools due to behavioral issues.

Alternative schools generally have stricter regulations and policies. When I attended, students were required to walk through metal detectors each morning as they were thoroughly searched. They were also required to wear uniforms and were not permitted to have bookbags. All classes were on one hallway and students were not permitted to roam around the school without adult supervision.

One day I, along with six of my classmates, decided to play a prank on our substitute teacher who'd left her cellphone on the desk while she repeatedly entered and left the classroom. We felt she needed to learn a lesson, specifically, for leaving her cellphone. We were classified as bad kids and we wanted to make sure she understood that.

The next time the substitute left the classroom, I took her cellphone off the desk and put it in my pocket. When she returned to the classroom, I told her I needed to use the bathroom. I went and played a few games then made a couple of calls with her phone. After enjoying a few minutes outside the classroom, I hid the phone under my clothes and returned. The teacher was in an uproar searching for her phone, while everyone else giggled and acted clueless as to what she was looking for.

When she left the room to inform the other teachers what had taken place and to inquire about what she needed to do, I returned the phone to her desk. She returned and found the phone unharmed however, she was still in an uproar. Later that day I was called to the office and expelled from school. My innocent joke cost me.

My mother didn't want me home alone every day so she and my dad both agreed I would go live with my aunt Angel in Atlanta. Towards the end of that summer I moved in with dad and his new wife. Although at the time, I didn't want to be reunited with him. I was enjoying my new life without him. Mom had lightened up on a lot of his strict rules and I didn't want to be confined to them again. At that time, I still held some resentment towards him for leaving me and for remarrying.

By then, dad had relocated to St. Louis and, against my wishes, my mother dropped me off at my aunts' house.

My aunt was short and plump. She didn't have any children of her own but she helped raise many others. She was the "go-to" woman in our family. Whether you needed a place to stay or a shoulder to lean on, one could always count on Auntie. She was talented, knowing how to cook, sew, and style hair very well. She worked for herself so she was at home all day and able to keep an eye on me to ensure I didn't find myself in any trouble.

Atlanta was great! As long as I completed my assignments, my aunt allowed me to do things neither of my parents ever allowed. My dad enrolled me in an online program that allowed me to get my diploma from home. I took a couple of hours each day to complete my assignments, then the work was submitted and graded by an online instructor. As long as I completed those daily assignments my aunt allowed me to go the skating rink with my cousins who, at the time, also lived in Atlanta.

The skating rink was the place to be on Saturday nights in Atlanta. It was often full of children from age 9 up to the mid-teens. Some people were actually there to skate but most of us were there to party and get our groove on. Children danced everywhere, from the skating rink floor to the walls of the rink. My cousins and I loved entering the dance contests. We hoped we'd win one day and actually came close a couple of times.

We spent weekdays at home watching the movie "Rize" and dancing. The movie was about a new dance move called Krumping. You would spread your legs apart, squat, and begin thrusting your hips in an upward motion as fast as you could. The people in the movie were very creative with it. Some of the actors/dancers wore clown outfits while others wore very skimpy cheerleader outfits made from home. Learning those dance moves became an everyday ritual for me.

As time went on, I began calling my Aunt's neighbors aunt and uncle as well. We spent nights dancing on their porch as the adults indulged in margaritas. We laughed, danced, and enjoyed memories. I enjoyed the liberty I experienced at my aunt's house. I wore whatever color nail polish I wanted, dyed my hair, and added long extensions. My aunt allowed me to try everything I wanted to try; something I was not permitted to when with my parents.

While in Atlanta something unexpected happened. One night my aunt came into my room and told me I was going to be arrested. She informed me there was a warrant for my arrest because the teacher, on whom I'd played the prank, pressed charges against me. My parents agreed that I would return to Warner Robins and turn myself.

After turning myself in I was bonded out and returned to live with my mom. She only agreed to me living with her because my probation was set in Warner Robins. Returning to familiar surroundings only made things worse, but in spite of all the negativity I did have a job. During that time, I was employed at a local Waffle House. Having a job gave me a lot of flexibility with my Mom. She never knew whether or not I was really at work. In reality, I was actually in a lot of places and doing a lot of things she never knew about; until I got pregnant.

One morning I went in to work my normal shift, being in great spirits I danced around the restaurant in anticipation of motherhood. I thought of how great a mother I would be. Then settled down for a moment to wash dishes when suddenly the phone rang. The conversation went as follows:

Me: "Thank you for choosing Waffle House! Did you need to place an order?"

Person on the other end of phone: "May I speak with Ashley?"

Me: "Speaking."

Person on the other end of phone: "Ashley Coklow?"

Me: "That's right. Who is this?"

Person on the other end of phone: "I'm your mother."

Me: "My mother?"

Person on the other end of phone: "Yeah, you know Josh and Gee Gee? That's your brother and your sister."

Me: "Yeah, those are my cousins' lady, not my brother and sister! Who is this? Is this some kind of joke?"

Person on the other end of phone: "No Ashley, I am your mother!"

Click (phone hangs up). I did not have time for whoever was playing on the phone. I was at work and had other things to do.

When I arrived home, I told my mother about the crazy lady who called playing a joke on me. My mom told me not to worry about it and tried to laugh it off but I could see the concern in her eyes. Something wasn't right but I was too tired to worry about it. I went to my room to get off my feet and dream about my new daughter, whom I was soon to meet.

Later that same night mom said, "Ashley, call your dad."

"No mom! I responded, I don't want to call him; we have nothing to talk about."

"Ashley, I am not asking you! I am telling you! Get on the phone and call your daddy!" mom said, frustrated and halfway yelling.

I did as she said, grunting to show my disapproval. The conversation went as follows:

Dad: "Ashley?"

Me: "Hey Dad."

Dad: "Cheri, are you there?"

Cheri (Mom): "Yes, I'm here," (using the house phone in her room).

I sat in the living room sensing something was up. Mom never forced me to talk to Dad when I didn't want to.

I questioned, why the three of us were on the phone together? This had never happened before. I waited in anticipation of what would happen.

Dad: "Ash, you were told something today at work. It is true. You are adopted."

Whoa! I could not believe my ears. Here I was eighteen years old and was just finding out I was adopted. I instantly, started rambling off numerous questions. I didn't know what to think or feel. I felt bad for having given my parents a hard time and being so disobedient yet grateful that somebody wanted me, even if my biological parents didn't. I recalled how my mom and dad had instilled in me the importance of being honest no matter what; yet I felt they'd lied to me all this time. I wondered who my biological mother was and what she was like.

My parents gave me her number and I called immediately.

"Hello!"

Me: "Hi! I'm Ashley Ciarro Coklow. Are you my mother?"

Divorce can be just as hard for children as it is for adults. Adults often forget that children are connected in the marriage as well. ***1 Corinthians 7:14*** says, ***"for the unbelieving husband is sanctified by the wife, and the unbelieving wife is sanctified by the husband: else were your children unclean; but now they are holy."*** In this scripture God shows us how children are connected to the marriage. The family is a unit.

Once a couple agrees to separate, the children who are involved should always be acknowledged and reassured because they often blame themselves for their parents' separation and divorce. A good idea is to sit down with them and explain what is taking place. Taking time to explain the situation to them will help them better understand so they are less likely to blame themselves. It is important to make sure children fully understand that they haven't done anything wrong.

Parents should avoid arguing in front of their children. Anger, frustration and hatred are emotions children can feel. Arguing in front of them can cause them to feel as though they need to pick sides. Furthermore, it is important that parents not use children as a pawn in disagreements or arguments. I recall being in school when my dad unexpectedly checked me out early. He took me to get pizza and we hung out that day. Later that evening he took me back to his apartment. I hadn't done anything special to earn the treatment I had gotten.

I later overheard my dad speaking with my mother over the phone. My mother requested that he bring me home because it was a school night but he declined her request because he wanted something from her and she was not consenting. He eventually took me home and I was saddened that I had to go because I missed him. I felt as though I needed to be on his side of the dispute between, he and my mother in order to receive similar treatment in the future. Afterall, we had a special relationship and he'd picked me up not my sister. During our phone calls I told him what I thought he wanted to hear. There were times when I even lied on my mother to make him happy.

During a divorce, it is important that the absent parents' love remain present. Frequent visits and phone calls help accomplish this. Couples should never allow differences between one another to dictate their relationship with their children. Throughout the process the child should never be left to wonder whether he or she is loved. They should be told and shown as often as possible.

It is important to understand and acknowledge that children may need help through their healing process. Purpose to help children adapt to their new environment without the absent parent. Their new environment should be a place of peace and joy. There can be peace and joy during the divorce process. Parents should make themselves available for their children to come and talk with them freely. Encourage them to communicate. Be approachable and frequently remind them that their marriage does not have to end the same way. Reassure them that they still have purpose.

If you are a victim of divorce, whether as a child or an adult, it is important to acknowledge that you may need help with your healing process. Regardless of how old you are or how many years ago it may have happened, you may still be in need of healing. I didn't realize this until my first attempt to write this book. My eyes welled with tears as I recalled certain things that took place.

If you are a victim of your parents' divorce and you are ready to begin the healing process, pray this prayer with me:

Dear God,

I come to you for healing. I ask you to heal every wound, every scar, and every hurt. Show me the root cause of my hurt and how to deal with it. Your word tells me to lean not to my own understanding, so I ask for your understanding in this situation. God you said to cast my cares upon you, because you care. I cast every care and every pain upon you. I release every situation and every person that caused me pain. I forgive those who never told me they were sorry and I forgive those who never realized they hurt me. I forgive my parents for not seeing me in the midst of their own storm. Thank you for loving me even when it felt like mom and dad didn't love me. Thank you for being there when it felt like no one else was. I believe that by your stripes I am healed and after this day, I will never be the same.

In the name of Jesus.

Amen

CHAPTER 2
Wild Child

My biological mother went into labor and gave birth to me while in the Ocala State Prison. During that time, she ran the streets, experimented with drugs, and found herself incarcerated during the time of my delivery. I was told that each time she discovered she was with child she would stop doing drugs and reside with her mother until it was time to deliver. While this may be true the risk of death, disease, and addiction to drugs is still a high risk for an unborn child. Her incarceration saved my life. Despite the doctors' belief that I was infected with HIV while in the womb, I was born healthy.

My biological mom had two other children, who were living with her mother, Big Ma. Big Ma was unable to care for me because she had health issues of her own and her hands full with the other two children. I lived with family members until Big Ma found someone to adopt me. That's when Cheri (mom) and Charles (dad) took me in. Cheri was Big Ma's sisters' daughter (my grandmothers' niece). I discovered I was adopted within my family. When I was taken in by Cheri and Charles, they changed my name. My sister and brother were not allowed to call me their sister so it wasn't until later that I learned they were my siblings.

We attended the same church but they were required to refer to me as their cousin. Family reunions and other gatherings were very painful to them because they were not permitted to develop the relationship with me as their sibling, they so desperately desired. My sister explained how she avoided me so that she would not be forced to keep the family secret. She described how painful it was to call me cousin knowing we were sisters. The pain was easier to manage with distance so she did her best to stay away.

Discovering I was adopted didn't impact me right away. I had numerous phone conversations with my biological mom prior to our first meeting. I discovered we resembled one another and had a lot in common. During our first visit she took me to the mall and bought me everything I wanted. She felt as though she owed me those things. She bought me Jordan's (shoes), and an outfit to match, she also got my hair done in the style I desired. Each time we met she would buy me something.

Sometimes, I'd call asking for things and she would send them to me.

As time progressed, I found myself wanting more and more from her. It got to a point where she had to tell me no and when she did, I'd become angry because I felt she owed me too. We didn't have a foundation. Our relationship was based solely on what I expected her to do. There is something to be learned here. Every relationship needs a solid foundation.

Matthew 16:18 says, "And I say unto thee, that thou art Peter, and upon this rock I will build my church; and the gates of hell shall not prevail against it." This scripture teaches us about building on a solid foundation. The word **"rock"** refers to someone or something that is extremely strong, reliable, or hard. A rock can withstand water, heat, snow or wind. Regardless of whether something is placed on top of it or taken away from it, the rock still remains. What are you building your relationships on? What are your relationships capable of enduring? The more solid your foundations are the more your relationships can endure. The previous scripture says even the gates of hell will not prevail against it. Is hell prevailing in your marriage? With your children? Your family members? …check your foundation.

My first pregnancy was planned with my boyfriend at the time, Casey. He was my first real boyfriend. Previous relationships consisted of passing notes in school. Outside of identifying one another as boyfriend and girlfriend, there was nothing that really defined us as such. Although none of them ever had vehicles, I had never been on a date because I was never allowed to leave the house with a male friend. Casey was different. He took me on dates, took me to work and picked me up from work. He and my mom knew one another and she thought he was a nice guy.

Casey was short and plump. I stood a couple of inches taller than he. He suffered from a limp as the result of a car accident that left him in a coma for weeks when he was a toddler. He didn't allow the injuries he sustained from the car accident to interfere with his dreams or his future. He was employed at Walmart and had recently graduated from high school. He was ambitious and had his own car at the time. He was doing well as a young man.

One day as we sat in my room, I told him I wanted to have a baby and questioned if he wanted to. He answered, "yes, I always wanted to have a baby." We never discussed how we would take care of or provide for the baby. As I reminisce, I can only speculate that I wanted to have a baby because I wanted a family of my own.

I obtained my GED just before giving birth to my daughter, Kayci. My dad was so proud of me that he bought me my first car. His only request was that I take care of it. Kayci and I stayed on the go. Shortly after I received the car, I decided it was time we and I got our own apartment. We had both been living with our parents long enough; it was time we became responsible adults and raised our own child.

Our first apartment was at a complex called Northlake Apartments. Although it was small, the two-story building had a living room, a kitchen, and a half bathroom down stairs. Upstairs, was a full bathroom and two bedrooms. Our goal was for Kayci to have her own room but she rarely slept in it.

I felt accomplished. I was living on my own, working a consistent job, and raising my daughter. I began to develop a callous attitude and acted as if I couldn't be told anything. I started hanging out with friends, sometimes, staying out all night. There were times when I didn't even come home to Casey and Kayci. I started going to clubs and meeting new friends. One of those new friends was Shaun. Tattoos covered her tanned brown body; she was so beautiful. Shaun literally had thousands of shoes and a surplus of clothes. I wanted what she had, so I questioned how I could get it.

"Where do you work?" I asked.

"I'm a dancer," she replied.

"Where do you dance?" I asked curiously.

"I'm an exotic dancer."

"Well, what is that?"

"I'm a stripper."

"Can you get me on?"

"Sure. Come up there today about 3:00 pm."

Later that day, I pulled up to a place called Neon; it was a small building. Large letters that spelled "Neon" hung across the slanted roof and there was a picture of a woman next to the sign. She had one leg up balancing herself on the other leg, as if she was dancing. She appeared to be taking off one of her dress straps as if to suggest she was undressing.

When I walked inside, I saw women everywhere who were barely wearing anything. Even the waitresses were barely clothed. I never realized a place like that was opened during the day. There was a Caucasian girl on the stage dressed in high boots that extended up to her thighs. Her little black skirt was so small it reminded me of a toddler's tutu for ballet. She was topless. Her black lipstick and dark eye shadow made me afraid of her. Yet the way she so elegantly moved as she gently danced around the pole made her appear harmless as drooling men stood around the stage watching at her. I saw twenty-dollar bills and one-dollar bills hit the floor as she winded her body and bent over. I had never been in a strip club before; to say I was amazed is stating it gently.

"Yo! What you need?" asked a deep voice breaking my daze.

"Uh-uh, I am looking for Lisa." I managed to stutter out of my mouth.

"I'm right here baby girl." said an old voice from a lady wearing glasses.

"I am here to apply."

"Right this way baby girl." she said, using her finger to summon me.

I followed her into a room with wall length mirrors on every wall in the room. In front of some of the mirrors was a countertop similar to that of a bathroom counter, but without a sink. Women sat in front of them applying their makeup and styling their hair. Others freely walked around naked. They practiced moves in the mirror and adjusted straps to make sure everything fit just right.

"Drop your clothes," Lisa said in an unfriendly voice. I hurriedly dropped my clothes and followed the commands given to me.

"Spin around. Bend over and touch your toes," in that same unfriendly voice.

"You start tonight; be here at 6:00 pm."

That is how the fast life began for me. Working at the strip club was the gateway which got me involved in sex, drugs, and fast money. When my name was called to go on stage for the first time, I was so scared that I was visibly shaking. Another stripper handed me a cigarette and said, "smoke this." It started with that one cigarette and expanded to illegal drugs and exposure to alcohol. I could not perform sober because of shame and humiliation so I stayed intoxicated to get the job done. I made unhealthy friendships while working at the club.

I moved out from my boyfriend, Casey, and got my own apartment where, at times, I allowed any and everybody to stay. When work was slow at the strip club, I began burglarizing peoples' houses along with the people who were living with me. I was also into gangs and guns. I believed they accepted me felt as though I finally fit in. In reality, they didn't accept me they only desired to use me. They were attracted to the things I had and the money I made. I later became pregnant by one of the guys who lived with me.

One evening, after a very productive day, we sat in the living room taking inventory of what we'd come up with during the course of that day. We had obtained two or three game systems, a couple of computers with monitors, and a couple of guns. We hit it big that day, collecting three thousand dollars in cash from one house! In celebration of our success we consumed bottles of alcohol and smoked marijuana. We danced around the living room as music loudly played.

As BJ, one of our house guests, examined one of the guns from the burglarized house it unintentionally went off just as Kayci danced around the living room. The bullet missed her by a hair. It scared me for a moment, but not enough to make me reconsider my lifestyle.

I was living close to death and didn't even realize it. The bible tells us that the wages of sin is death. God loves us so much! He covered me even when I didn't have a mind to pray for or protect myself or my daughter. I turned my back on God for the temporary fulfilment of sin. I turned my back on God for the acceptance of others; which became a long-term necessity for validation from others.

I lived that lifestyle until I was incarcerated for nearly a year. Being incarcerated only brought about a temporary change and a corrupt mindset. I was exposed to other inmates who led me to believe I could be smarter in future crimes. I gave birth to my second daughter within a week of being released from jail. I returned to my old lifestyle and began a cycle of going back and forth to jail. My mom had remarried by that time. She had done her job of raising me and didn't deserve having to put up with and entertain my shenanigans. I realized I was on my own and homeless.

CHAPTER 3
Toxic Relationship

My daughters lived with their father's while I worked to gain stability. By then, I was pregnant with my third child and living from pillar to post. I had moved from shelter to shelter and exhausted all my resources. My unborn child's father, Billy, weathered the storm with me. Billy was a former classmate with whom I'd attended alternative school. He and I had remained friends throughout the years. He visited me while I was hospitalized during my previous pregnancy. It was a low point in my life and he was there for me.

We began dating from that point on. Billy and I spent the days figuring out where we would lay our heads each night. We spent hours at the hospital until we were asked to leave. We found places to hang out that were open for 24 hours until we could secure a place to sleep. Some nights we slept in his car, a 1997 black and yellow Crown Victoria.

While applying for assistance at the local county office, one of the workers expressed her concern about my living arrangements. Instead of calling the proper authorities to have my children taken, which is what she was supposed to do, she gave me the phone number of a woman named Mrs. Bell. Mrs. Bell secured a hotel room for me to live in for a week, but she told me I could not allow Billy to stay there with me. I was disobedient.

Each night, when darkness fell, I would sneak him in. We continued this for a couple of nights until Mrs. Bell told me she was taking me to the Salvation Army in Macon, which was about thirty minutes away. She said she needed the room for another young lady who didn't have anywhere to go. Billy was angry and insisted I stay. I didn't want to go but I packed my bags and we left.

Upon arriving I was immediately reminded of jail. There were locked doors everywhere. The attendant informed us that I would have to sleep on a mat on the floor. The rooms were similar to that of a jail in that they only contained bunk beds. Each day, I was required to leave and return to the shelter by a certain time. I was informed I could bring my children with me once I produced their social security cards and birth certificates. The program was intended to provide me with shelter until I found a job and was financially able to get my own place to live. Mrs. Bell left me there with one book bag. I informed her I would get the rest of my things later. I thanked her for everything and we said our goodbyes.

As she drove away, I placed a call.

"Hello," I said

"Hey Ashley. Why did you leave? How is that saying that you love me?" Billy asked.

"I don't want to be here either. This place reminds me of jail and I miss you," I said almost crying.

"Just leave, and come back."

"Where are we going to stay if I come back?" I asked with concern.

"Don't worry about it. Just come on. I got you."

I believed him. I left with my book bag and started walking a twenty-mile journey. I was eight months pregnant, but I didn't care. I didn't like where I was and I wanted to be with Billy. I walked until darkness fell; by then I had made it to Warner Robins, but my legs couldn't take anymore. I stopped at a gas station; which was the safest thing to do, since it was dark. I asked the driver of every car that came and left if they could give me a lift. Finally, a man and his girlfriend agreed to give me a lift because they were headed to Warner Robins and they were going to pass the hotel I was going to. Billy had gotten his dad to give him money for a hotel for two nights.

I made it back to Billy. He was still angry with me for leaving him. His silence was my punishment. We discussed our plans for the next day and went to sleep. The next morning, I went to my class at the Department of Family and Children Services office. To receive financial assistance from their office I was required to attend class on Monday through Friday. They'd send a van to pick me up and drop me off each day if transportation was needed. Billy and I agreed that he would walk me to the location where the van would pick me up and he would be there when the van returned to drop me off.

The class lasted from 9am until 12noon. I could hardly wait to get out of class and be back with Billy. Although he wasn't working at the time and didn't really have anything going for himself, I saw potential in him. My parents were not very fond of him, but it didn't matter what others thought of our relationship. All that mattered was that he loved me. He had been there during the lowest points in my life.

When I returned from class, Billy wasn't waiting for me as we'd agreed. I assumed he was in the room sleeping. After pounding on the door for several minutes without an answer, I went to the front desk and requested a key to the room. The attendant informed me that Billy had checked out of the room. Various thoughts ran through my mind as I sat in the front lobby. I had nowhere to go and I didn't have a clue where Billy was; he wouldn't answer his phone. I couldn't comprehend what was happening.

I decided to call his mother. She was always kind and honest with me about him. When she answered, she informed me that Billy had left for Atlanta earlier that day and that he would be living there with his sister. I was furious! I was angry with him and with myself. I sat in the lobby of the hotel and wept. I didn't know what I was going to do or where I would go. I had no one to call and I'd used all of my resources. I could see how God had provided me with an escape from the situation but I didn't take it because it was a new, unfamiliar, and uncomfortable place.

I chose to go back to a familiar place. I went back into my comfort zone. There is something to be learned here. Don't reject the new thing God is trying to do with you because it is unfamiliar or uncomfortable to you. He may send help or provide you a way out of your situation but, if not careful, you might reject him because of the new or unfamiliar. Don't reject the new thing God is trying to do with you!

This is my encouragement to everyone who may be on a destructive path or is considering one. Put your hope and trust in God! Don't look to people for help. Man will fail you every time. *"Put not your trust in princes, nor in the son of man, in whom there is no help" (Psalms 146:3).*

That same day, I walked and walked and walked, because I had nowhere to go. I ended up walking to Ada Lee Park; it was clean and very well-kept with a couple of slides, and swings for the children to play on. I watched as children played while their parents smiled on. One mother waited anxiously at the bottom of the slide for her daughter to return to her. I longed for my mother; not just my mother but my family. The slide is symbolic of our relationship with Christ. He releases us to make our own choices in life but we don't know what bumps life will present to us or how those bumps will affect us.

Sometimes, we are like a child on a slide. . . scared because we are temporarily alone. Other bumps in life may bring us to laughter. But as always, when the child is reunited with his/her parent at the bottom of the slide there is hugging, joy, and security. No matter what bumps we may experience in life, the Father is patiently awaiting our return.

I was at the very bottom of my slide and I needed God. I waited for all the parents and children to leave then, after park hours, I drifted off to sleep. It had been a long hot day, but when the sun went down it cooled nicely. Shortly thereafter, my sleep was abruptly interrupted as I was awakened to a group of cats encircling the bench I was sleeping on. I was terrified, because I have a fear of cats. They stared at me, purring and growling, as if I had something to give them. I can only speculate that since I was with child and close to delivery, they were most likely after the milk I carried.

That night, I called out to God because I had nowhere else to turn. Sometimes God will allow us to position ourselves in a place where we can only look up. Choose him first. You'll receive His grace and he will get the glory. Sometimes God uses the difficult situations we experience in life to draw us closer to Him. . . if we are receptive. God answered my prayer! That night was my last night sleeping outside.

The next morning, when the park restroom was unlocked, I washed up and hitched hiked a ride to class. I met a woman there who opened her home to me until I could find my own place. She provided me with transportation whenever I needed to get to class or a doctor's appointments. Sometimes she allowed my other two daughters to come visit; even allowing them to stay over some nights. She granted me full access to her house and the refrigerator. I could eat whenever I was hungry.

While residing there, I delivered another baby girl and shortly thereafter I was provided an apartment in Perry, GA through the Perry Housing Authority. After being separated from my daughters for a little over a year, we were finally reunited and all living under one roof.

My relationship with Billy was toxic. A toxic relationship is unhealthy and can be destructive for one or both parties involved. The first step to being free from a toxic relationship is to identify you are in one. Signs of a toxic relationship include jealousy, possessiveness, dominance, manipulation, desperation, selfishness, and rejection. This is not Gods' way nor is it his desire.

If you are in a toxic relationship and are desiring to be free pray this prayer with me:

Dear God,

I acknowledge I am in a relationship that is not pleasing to you and I acknowledge that it is not healthy for me. I ask for your help and your strength to be freed from this relationship. I ask you to sever every stronghold and every soul tie. Destroy the yoke of bondage and everything that has held me bound. I release my will to be in this relationship. I believe that whom you have made free is free indeed. After this day I will no longer be confined to this relationship.

In the name of Jesus.

Amen

CHAPTER 4
Perry Housing Authority

The Perry Housing Authority is an income-based housing that is funded by the government. They had approximately 20-25 apartment buildings which were fenced in. They also had a park in the complex where children played. There, everyone knew one another and, for the most part, everyone was friendly. Children rode bikes throughout the neighborhood and played games like tag and hide and seek. The apartment complex was comprised of people who were gossipers, fighters, and troublemakers. Nevertheless, I made solid friends in the neighborhood and started attending church with them.

Endia was one of my new-found friends. She was still in high school but she was the first friend I made in that neighborhood. She lived in an apartment across the street from me along with her mother and step dad Devarrus. She and her mother took me in from the first time we met. They treated me and my daughters like family. Endea's mom, Viv, assisted with everything she could possibly assist with. Including rides, babysitting, and food.

One of the things that drew Endia & I together was the fact that she loved music and could really sing. Listening to her sing was like watching a waterfall; she had the voice of an angel.

One day, she and I returned from singing at a local nursing home and as we all sat around laughing and talking about our experience, we heard a knock on the door.

"Hey, is Devarrus here?" said a handsome voice.

"No, he's not," Endia said.

I was curious about the mysterious person. He was a little taller than I was and had a honey brown complexion. He also had a tattoo over his right eye which may have indicated he was in a gang. He wore a red and white Chuck Taylor gang shirt and jeans. I was immediately attracted to the fact that he was possibly in a gang.

"Who was that?" I excitedly asked.

"Oh nobody, my cousin," she said nonchalantly.

"Tell him I want to talk to him," I said.

"Girl for real? You talking about my cousin Travis?" she asked.

"Yes." I said with a serious face.

"Okay I gotcha. I'm for real nie," she said.

"Okay I'm for real nie," I said.

At that point in my life I was stable, working a minimum wage job at Pizza Hut, and doing very well. I was caring for my three daughters, taking them to church, and I was attending school. For the most part, my family was pleased with my progress. It was then that I decided I was ready for a new relationship.

"Ashley! Oh my gosh! Travis texted you!" said Endia with excitement. I was driving and, as always, she had my phone.

"What does it say?" I said just as excited.

"Girl, it says what you doing wife?" she said putting emphasis on wife.

"Okay just text him back for me." I replied.

Most of the time when someone texted my phone, they would actually be having a conversation with Endia. The majority of the time I never knew about the conversation. We were around each other so much that she would often finish my sentences and say what I was thinking.

Endia set me up to meet Travis at his mother's house later that day. She attended the same church I did and lived in the same apartment complex. I knew almost all of Travis's family but never knew he existed. I was actually very close friends with his sister. She babysat my children from time to time but never once told me she had a brother, and I never saw him while visiting their mothers' house.

One night, Travis decided to cook for me. Food is definitely the way to my heart. After eating we cuddled, listened to music, had a couple of drinks, and he smoked. That night he ended up spending the night. Being with him made me feel good. I was ready to be loved again. It felt good to be loved, held, and kissed. My heart was warmed watching him interact with the children. From that night on Travis never left...my home became our home. I felt like I had a family because his family accepted me as if I was their own.

After my encounter with Christ at Ada Lee Park, I began desiring more of a relationship with Jesus. I knew of him because of my childhood and upbringing but I didn't have my own personal relationship with him. Travis did not want a relationship with Christ. I did not realize the negative impact living with someone who was unequally yoked could have on my relationship with Christ. My relationship with Travis became detrimental to my relationship with Christ.

Friends tried to warn me of his past and the possibility of the relationship not being the best fit for me. I did not heed the advice given to me. I felt as if they didn't know him the way I did. I thought if I was good to him, he would be good to me.

Being re-exposed to things I had been freed from caused me to miss those things and I eventually returned to them. When you are a babe in Christ it is best to separate yourself from things that you were delivered from. We often hear people say, "Jesus ate with sinners." However, we forget the scripture reminding us not to be unequally yoked. We forget the scripture that tell us light has no fellowship with darkness.

In **2 Corinthians 6:17**, the bible says, **"Wherefore come out from among them, and be ye separate, saith the Lord, and touch not the unclean thing: and I will receive you."** I love the latter part of this scripture which says, "and I will receive you." God is not rejecting us, oftentimes he's just not accepting what we choose to remain connected to. First, he commands us to **"come out."** Then he tells us to **"be separate."** That means to be different. This may mean you will be alone at times. Then he then commands us to **"touch no unclean thing."** Once you have been made clean don't contaminate yourself again by touching that which is unclean.

With new born babies, we do everything we can to make sure things are sterile because we don't want the baby to get infected or sick; they are so small and their immune systems are not as strong as an adult's. This correlates to our relationship with Christ. When we are new in Christ it is important to stay clear of things that could cause us to get sick or lead to spiritual death.

I was not able to identify the relationship with Travis as a form of lust. I was still broken and had a distorted view of things. I hadn't healed from my previous hurts. While the relationship with my family was getting better, we were still estranged. The relationship with Travis was an opportunity to feel loved and I accepted it. We appeared to be a happy couple and for the most part we were.

Travis smoked synthetic marijuana; on occasion I would smoke it as well. In the city where we lived it was called "trippy." Probationers smoked trippy instead of marijuana because it didn't intoxicate you due to it not containing THC. Because there an absence of THC it allowed people to successfully pass drug tests with no suspicion of substance abuse. Probationers could still enjoy feeling intoxicated without risking their freedom. However, because this substance was man-made it was very dangerous. There had been numerous reports of deaths and serious injuries within our local area, including with people we personally knew. Nonetheless, smoking trippy was a daily ritual for Travis.

As our relationship progressed Travis' desire for trippy increased. As long as he remained high, we had no problems. When I couldn't afford trippy, he'd lash out at me, often leaving home for days without telling me where he was going or when he would return. He was verbally abusive and also became physically abusive.

One night, I learned Travis had been cheating in our relationship. His friends were over that night, which was normal; they were always there. During the majority of our relationship we always had at least one of his friends living with us. I supported everyone because neither he nor his friends worked. I supplied cigarettes for everyone so the house was always filled with smoke and people. Parties were always held at my expense.

That same night, I decided to question him about his mistress when his friends stepped outside. He lied at first, and when he realized I had his phone he became infuriated and slapped me. We tussled over the phone for a few minutes until I relinquished it; my strength was no match for his. The fact that I had given up the phone was not enough for him. His friends watched as he jerked me around the living room. When I threatened to call the police, his friends left.

At that point we were in the house alone with the children who were in the back room with the door closed. When I was able to get free, I ran into my bedroom and hid in the closet but somehow, he was able to bypass the locked door. He snatched me from the closet and yanked me onto the bed. This time he had a gun. It was a long wooden rifle. He held me down while holding the rifle to my face with his other hand. I stared at the barrel of it shaking violently. As I continued to wail and cry out the girls ran into the room.

They began crying as well. They stood there but said nothing. One of them girls left the room and ran to get Travis' sister, who was next door. His aunt also lived next door to us. Moments later, his sister Mesha ran through the door pleading with Travis to put the gun down but he wouldn't. Her tears went unnoticed. Mesha called their mom and explained what was happening. At her mother's request she handed Travis the phone.

As he spoke with his mom. I repeatedly heard him tell her I wanted to break up with him and that I was going to leave him. He explained to her that I couldn't leave him. He told his mother that I had to stay with him forever. Moments after talking to his mother, he moved the gun away from my head. His mothers' words had calmed him down. He put the gun back into the closet and went outside. His sister tended to my wounds and helped me calm the girls down. Then I threatened the children by telling them they had better not say anything to anyone about what happened.

The next day, the girls went to the school and told their teachers what happened. They told their teachers they were scared and they didn't want to go home. I received a phone call in regards to what they'd expressed but I lied. I always lied for Travis. I advised them not to be alarmed and to disregard the information but in reality, things were spiraling out of control. I was scared of Travis. At times, I'd jump when he simply walked by. I felt as though I had to do whatever he requested to keep him from being angry with me. I wanted to leave but I was scared at the possibility that, if I tried, I may not live to tell the story.

As time progressed, Travis learned through observation that the drug dealer was interested in me. He began using me as a pawn to get trippy from Arnold (the dealer). He'd have me to text and flirt with Arnold. At first it was friendly messages geared only at getting trippy but the more I opened up to Arnold the more he opened up to me. There were times when he wouldn't serve Travis if I wasn't with him. I could tell Arnold really liked me and I liked him too. He eventually gave me a different number to contact him on than the one his clients used. Sneaking around with Arnold became exciting. We eventually fell in love with one another.

CHAPTER 5
Content with Contempt

Arnold was a tall, dark-skinned, handsome man. He was baldheaded with a muscular build, and had long black eyelashes which added to his adorableness. At the time, he was in his late 30s and had a few golds in his mouth. He owned a black truck; which he loved and always wore a do-rag or a polo hat. He was never caught without something on his head. Arnold worked for the city of Perry and was very involved with his children. He also had a girlfriend who worked at the local hospital. Together, they shared a nice home in Perry.

The more Arnold and I opened up to one another about our relationships and the things we were experiencing the more we fell in love. We'd talk all day while he worked and when his girlfriend went to work her shift at the hospital, we'd talked all night. He made me feel as though I was the only one. I was able to both see and talk with him whenever I wanted to. There were many nights we spent at the Holiday Inn; we called it our second home. It was our secret meeting place.

Sometimes he paid, sometimes I paid. It felt good not having to support everyone all the time. Arnold took care of me, the girls, and Travis too.

I remember riding to Perry with Travis and the girls one day and we got a flat tire. We didn't have a spare or money to tow the car. We were stranded so I called Arnold. Without asking questions he came, brought a tire, and put it on while Travis watched. There were multiple times when he came to my rescue but he never gave Travis the slightest idea that we were involved. I was just as respectful around his girlfriend. As a matter of fact, our children often ended up playing on the same recreational team so I'd see her often. I would wave at and hug her as if nothing was going on between me and Arnold.

Sneaking around became exciting for us. We joked about the two and how naïve they were. We laughed at how foolish they were for not loving us like they should have and letting us slip away. Although he never agreed to leave his girlfriend; I never asked him to. He never asked me to leave Travis and, likewise, I never agreed to. We were both in relationships we didn't want to be in but we also knew we weren't going to leave them. Arnold and I became comfortable with one another. We started going to public places together. On occasion, I even rode with him to make drug deals.

We never had an argument; I can't even recall being mad at him once. People started suspecting we had something going on but we'd rebuttal everything. We were loyal to one another, as if we were the only one in each other's life. I was okay with not being his girlfriend and happy being his side chick. Eventually, he began taking advantage of my loyalty and exerting too much control over me. I eventually left Travis to be with him.

At the time, I did not understand my worth so I remained in a secret relationship with him for years. I didn't understand I was bought with a price and was selling myself short. I was content with being contempt.

One day while on the way to church, I received a phone call.

"Hello" I answered.

"May I speak with Ashley?" the caller asked.

"This is me. What's up?"

"Ashley, Travis is not breathing. He is not responding!" The caller said frantically.

"Where is he?" I asked out of concern.

"On the way to Houston Medical Center."

"I'm on my way there." I said

Although I'd left Travis, I still loved and deeply cared for him. I cancelled my engagement that night and rushed to the hospital. When I arrived, I learned he had been smoking trippy. All the chemicals he'd consumed damaged his body. His mother and family were there but no one greeted me upon my arrival. I thought it was strange because his family had never acted that way towards me. Nevertheless, I waited in the hospital lobby to see what was to come.

I watched as various family members walked back; I could only assume they were going to visit him. I patiently waited to be called back to visit with him, but around 10pm, his family members began leaving. After everyone had left the hospital, I walked up to the nurse's station and asked if I could go back to visit with Travis. The nurse informed me the family had placed a code on his room and only people with that code were permitted in the room. After making a couple of phone calls in an attempt to get the code, I was informed that Travis' mother didn't want anyone going into the room.

I was upset and questioned why she would keep him from me. After all, I had been the one who'd cared for him. I was the one with whom he'd lived and I had never done anything to harm him. Nevertheless, I was not permitted to visit him while he was hospitalized. I stayed in contact with his sister, checking his status on a daily basis. She informed that he was in a coma and they didn't know if or when he would pull through.

Later that same day, I visited with my adoptive mother and my step-dad, Don. He was a man full of wisdom. I went to him whenever I needed spiritual guidance. He was always able to discern when something was wrong with me, even when I didn't speak or show it. Don advised me not to be mad with Travis' mother because of her decision not to allow me to see him. He explained that this was my chance to be totally delivered from that relationship. He advised me to stay away from the hospital and let God work on him while he was there. He further explained that God not only wanted to work on him but also wanted to work on me. He shared that becoming involved would cause me to be entangled with the yoke of bondage again.

Sunday morning of that same week I decided to press my way to church. I was worried about Travis but I didn't want worry to consume me. I recall being in the middle of praise and worship when I received a text saying that Travis had awakened and was asking for me. Instead of taking heed to my step dad's words, I rushed to the hospital to be by his side.

Once I arrived, I found his sister Mesha, there waiting for me and she took me back to see Travis. I explained why he was there but he didn't believe me. He refused to believe that smoking trippy had caused his condition. He blamed for being cruel to him and told me he became sick and fainted because I did not respond to his texts and requests for rides. Even on his sick bed he was cold and mean. For a brief second, I regretted I cared so much and had taken the time to visit him.

He was released from the hospital and, because he did not believe his condition was caused by trippy, he smoked it again and was readmitted to the hospital. This time his family did not restrict me from accessing his hospital room. I visited him daily, singing to him, and praying over him while he slept. This time when he awakened from his coma, he believed trippy to be the cause and vowed not to smoke it again. We agreed to commit to one another and give each other a 2nd chance. From that point we resumed our relationship.

I'd like to pause to discuss a major issue: Engaging in a relationship with someone who is already in a relationship is a major issue. Let's visit the story of the Samaritan woman.

7 There cometh a woman of Samaria to draw water: Jesus saith unto her, Give me to drink.

8 (For his disciples were gone away unto the city to buy meat.)

9 Then saith the woman of Samaria unto him, how is it that thou, being a Jew, askest drink of me, which am a woman of Samaria? for the Jews have no dealings with the Samaritans.

10 Jesus answered and said unto her, if thou knewest the gift of God, and who it is that saith to thee, give me to drink; thou wouldest have asked of him, and he would have given thee living water.

11 The woman saith unto him, Sir, thou hast nothing to draw with, and the well is deep: from whence then hast thou that living water?

12 Art thou greater than our father Jacob, which gave us the well, and drank thereof himself, and his children, and his cattle?

13 Jesus answered and said unto her, whosoever drinketh of this water shall thirst again:

14 But whosoever drinketh of the water that I shall give him shall never thirst; but the water that I shall give him shall be in him a well of water springing up into everlasting life.

15 The woman saith unto him, Sir, give me this water, that I thirst not, neither come hither to draw.

16 Jesus saith unto her, Go, call thy husband, and come hither.

17 The woman answered and said, I have no husband. Jesus said unto her, thou hast well said, I have no husband:

18 For thou hast had five husbands; and he whom thou now hast is not thy husband: in that saidst thou truly.

John 4:7-18 (KJV)

While researching, I was unable to find anything in scripture that provided a reason as to why the Jews disliked the Samaritans. It became clear to me that the Samaritan woman herself may not have known why the Jews had no dealings with Samaritans. Her statement was based on what she had been told and taught.

Forgetting her own identity, she grouped herself amongst people who came from the same place she did. "The Jews have no dealings with the Samaritans." We know that's what the Samaritans believed, but what do you believe? We know that's what the Samaritans did, but what do you do? Even though Jesus asked her a question, she did not separate herself from the group.

Sometimes we go through things without separating ourselves from what happened to us in the past. We don't separate ourselves from things our parents and grandparents did. We don't separate ourselves from past traumas. As a result we begin to identify ourselves with those things and, if not checked, they become our identity.

For example:
 I was born in prison, so I'll die in prison. My daddy doesn't want me so nobody does.
My mom was nothing, I'm going to be nothing.
I was raped, so I'm used goods, I'm good for nobody.

I made bad choices, so I'll never get a good job.

While reading this scripture, I initially thought about her statement. She stated the Jews have no dealings with the Samaritans, but do the Samaritans have dealings with married men?" In that moment God spoke to me and said, "just as the first statement was a result of what she was accustomed to, so was the second statement." Those broken relationships were normal to her.

Broken relationships became my normality and it all stemmed from the broken relationship I experienced with my family. I lived with brokenness for so long that it was my normality. Just as the Samaritan woman, I didn't see anything wrong with my actions. Jesus acknowledged that she had five husbands, none of whom were hers. The text does not indicate that she was embarrassed or afraid. She did not try to hide it or lie about it; neither did she ask for forgiveness.

In *verse 15,* the woman asks Jesus to, *"give her this water that she would thirst not."* She knew committing adultery was only a quick fix until she was thirsty again. Previously, she'd tried to quench her thirst with the wrong thing. Have you ever drunk a soda and still been just as thirsty afterwards? That's because your body needed water. Your body needs water but your desire is for soda. Instead of drinking the water you need, you resolve to drink soda. As a result, you become thirsty again.

We see this same concept illustrated here. She needed healing but she kept chasing her desires. Which may have been love from a man, pleasure, or money. As a result, the cycle continued because she wasn't receiving the healing she so desperately needed. The living water Jesus provides will cause you to thirst no more.

If you are ready to declare broken relationships will no longer be your normality, pray this prayer with me:

Dear God,

Create in me a clean heart and renew a right spirit within me. Renew my mind Lord, so I may be transformed. Thank you that my thoughts about myself are changing now. Thank you that I will no longer succumb to others' normality. I confess with my mouth that you are Lord. I repent of everything I've done that was not pleasing to you. I believe I am a new creature.

In the name of Jesus, I pray,

Amen

CHAPTER 6
From This Day Forward

After Travis was released from the hospital, I did not allow him to live with me again, although we did resume our relationship. He'd made promises to change but I wanted to see whether he was being truthful or if he just trying to win me over. Each Sunday we began attending church together. He began taking interest in things I had interest in and showed signs he wanted the same things out of life I did. He became just as sweet as he was when we first met. He was a totally different person when he was clean and not using trippy. He left the drugs alone and I left the drug dealer alone.

I allowed Travis to move back in with me after a couple of weeks. He had gotten a job and was helping out with the responsibilities which were designated to him. One day, while at church, the pastor communicated to Travis that I was his wife. Travis and I looked at each other and thought it was funny because we had not considered marriage up to that point. The pastor began questioning us as to why we had not gotten married. He asked what we were waiting for. We glanced at one another again then began mumbling excuses such as, "we don't know if we were ready," and "we don't have the funds for a wedding." The pastor had a rebuttal for every excuse we presented. He began to tell us that he would help us with wedding and all we had to was set a date. So, we did.

Instead of waiting to see if Travis's changes were permanent, I made plans to marry him. My aunt, with whom I'd previously lived, helped us plan the wedding. She took care of the food, decorations, and made my daughters' dresses. I would wear my mother's old wedding dress. My father and his wife would come down from Virginia and take care of any expenses that were not accounted for.

The morning of my wedding, I left home early because I didn't want Travis to see me getting dressed. I was going to get dressed at the church; both my sister and my aunt would help me. Travis and his best man, Joe, were supposed to be at home getting dressed for the wedding but when I returned home unexpectedly, I found Travis sitting in a chair slumped over. He was so out of it that he didn't even realize I had walked up to him and opened his hand to see a small baggie of trippy. I was devasted. Travis was high. He smelled of trippy and his eyes were red. What was supposed to be a special day was starting off on the wrong track.

I fussed at Travis and every person who was in the house that day. I knew then that I didn't want to marry him. I didn't know how long he had been smoking behind my back but I knew when he smoked trippy he was not able to function. I was too embarrassed to cancel the wedding. I didn't want to upset my family members who had traveled from out of town. I feared my family's effort to make this day special for me were in vain. I remember walking down the aisle telling myself I was making a mistake.

As I continued down the aisle, I could see that Travis' eyes were red. The audience thought he had been crying. Right before entering the church and walking down the aisle my aunt came to the back where I was getting dressed to tell me he had been crying. When I was able to see him, I realized what was really going on. He was as high as a kite and could barely stand at the altar. His best man, Joe, was practically propping him up. He swayed back and forth as if his knees were going to buckle at any moment. The guests didn't recognize his behavior but I did. The closer I got to him the more disappointed I became.

My dad was our photographer, and as Travis and I took pictures together, I said all kinds of mean things to him through my teeth, all while forcing a smile. I said things to him like, "I hate you, I really didn't want to marry you, and how could you ruin this day." No one around us was able to tell what was going on or that I was considering this to be one of the worst days of my life.

During our reception, as we sat at the honoree table, he kept falling face forward. I kept picking him up and nudging him to stay awake. We didn't dance together or celebrate as normal newlyweds do. We cut our wedding cake, I gave a speech of thanks and gratitude, then I let him sleep. He slept the remainder of the reception, waking just long enough to walk to the car when the reception was finished. When we returned home, Joe had to carry him in the house where he slept for the rest of the day. He never touched me that night.

Joe, whom we'd brought home with us spent the night. The next day, I tried to wake Travis up for church but he wouldn't wake up. I called his mother to see if I should call 911. His mother told me to bring him to church so she could see him. I dressed him and his best friend put him in the car. He was awake but he moved was as if he was sleep walking, dragging his feet while trying to walk. He was also drooling and foaming at the mouth. When we arrived at the church and his mother saw his condition, she instructed me to take him to the hospital if he had not come out of his trance in a couple of hours. I took him back home and he slept the remainder of the day.

That following morning, I woke Travis up to get ready for work. He was moving a lot better but still appeared drowsy and was barely able to dress himself. I drove him to work and as he was getting out of the car, I noticed his pants were hanging off and his under shorts were visible. I tried to tell him to fix his clothes but he refused. I watched as he stumbled into work, wondering how productive he would be considering his condition.

I got about five minutes down the road when my phone rang. It was Travis calling for me to come back and pick him up. His supervisor thought he was drunk and sent him home. We later learned that he was terminated and not permitted to return. We were back at square one again. He didn't have a job and I was back to taking care of him and his friends. His addiction to trippy increased. This time, he did not try to hide it. He stopped attending church and began walking the streets again. Things were going downhill quickly.

I continued to attend church even though he wouldn't go with me. I was committed to God. When we married and my life lined up with Gods will for my life, my relationship with God began to grow. I took instructions from God concerning my husband and my marriage. I didn't fuss at him for not having a job or paying bills, and I didn't become angry when he walked the streets late at night or when I returned home and couldn't find him. I didn't complain when I came home to a dirty house. I remained silent and prayed for him and our marriage.

One day I sat in my car outside our home; Travis was in the back of the house sleeping. It was common for me to sit outside in the car and listen to music; especially while he slept. That particular day, I noticed he'd left his phone in my car. I picked it up and decided to go through it while sitting in the car. Travis quickly came through the drivers' side and began choking me. I immediately dropped the phone and began yelling, "I don't have it, I don't have it," but it didn't matter; he wouldn't stop. I felt his teeth dig into the back side of my hand as I tried to fend him off. Sometime afterwards I blacked out.

I awakened to my children running up to the car as they happily yelled, "mommy!" They had just gotten off the bus. I noticed Travis was nowhere to be found and Joe was standing on the porch. I wondered how much of the attack he had witnessed. It was not uncommon for his friends to watch him attack me. The children had no knowledge of what had just taken place. I took them in the house, they changed out of their school clothes, and began their homework.

I realized I was bleeding and that Travis did not need to get away with his actions, so I decided to call the police. Just as he was returning from wherever he had been. He questioned why I had called the police but I refused to answer any of his questions. I wanted my silence to speak louder than my words. After I refused to respond, Travis called his aunt and began to telling her he needed a ride because I had called the police on him. He continued and told her I was ruining his life and trying to send him back to jail. His aunt sent her fiancé to pick him up.

He arrived just before the police did and spoke with Travis outside while his aunt talked with me. She began explaining that I was ruining Travis' life and that it wasn't good that he be locked up. She told me we were married and that we needed to work things out. I allowed her to make me feel guilty; as though I had done wrong by calling the police. She convinced me that doing so was not the best solution to the problem.

The police called me back and asked if had I called them. They explained the reason they had not already arrived was because they needed the house number. I lied and told them I had not called. Moments later, police knocked on my door. By that time Travis' uncle had left and he was back in the room motioning for me to get rid of them. I cracked the front door slightly, being careful not to let them see any bruising or blood. They asked if I had called the police. I told them I had not. I can only imagine that the streaks of dried tears and scratches on my face indicated I was lying because they questioned me three times before they left. I repeatedly told them no.

The abuse continued as Travis' behavior worsened. I told no one that I could barely pay my bills, had an abusive husband, or that my life was spiraling out of control. I didn't fight back physically, I fought in prayer. I told God my problems, cried out to him, and continued with my life attending church, school, and work as if nothing was wrong. There were days when I cried but, before entering my workplace, church, or school, I dried my tears and cleaned my face. I didn't let anyone around me know I was in serious warfare at home.

The church I attended at the time was holding a 31-day revival. They attended church every day during the month of December. During that time, I was working two different jobs and attending to school. I would check in one job at 10:00 am and get off at 7 pm. As soon as I was off from that job, I would go straight to the revival. I'd leave church between 9:30-10:00 pm and go straight to my second job where I'd work until 6:00 am the next morning. Then I'd return home to get the girls ready for school.

By the time I was done with them I'd only have about an hour to sleep before I had to begin the morning job, which started at 10 am. I spent a lot of time away from home. In the early years of our relationship I'd only worked part-time and did not attend church so he wasn't used to me spending that much time away from home. As my relationship with Christ grew, I attended church more consistently but I'd never attended that much or spent that much time away from home.

On the last night of the revival, Travis was beyond frustrated with me. He'd had enough. Throughout the entire service that night, he sent threatening text messages, accusing me of cheating and lying. When my responses were delayed, he grew angrier. Instead of going to work that night, I went straight home after church.

When I arrived home, I went straight to bed and Travis came right behind me, jumped on top of me, and snatched my phone. His breath smelled heavily of liquor. He had been drinking and I knew he was drunk. When he didn't find what he was looking for in the phone he began yelling obscenities at me. He called me names and said hateful things. I was still overwhelmed from the great time I'd had at church. I refused to let anything get me down. I didn't react to his hateful outbursts. As a matter of fact, I didn't say anything at all. That frustrated him even more. Sometimes silence is more powerful than spoken words.

As he left the room, he stated I was only good for sleeping with Arnold; that sparked a fire in me. I jumped off of the bed and followed him as he walked into the living room. He sat on the couch and played on his phone as if I was invisible. I snatched his phone to get his attention. As soon as the phone was in my possession, I realized I had made a mistake. Within the blink of an eye, he had tackled me to the ground. I released the phone as a sign of surrender but he didn't stop. I verbally acknowledged no longer having the phone but he didn't let up.

The girls were so disturbed by the noise they'd stopped playing and come to see what was going on. They immediately began crying when they saw Travis on top of me. I begged him to stop hitting me for the girls' sake. My strength was no match for his so I'd learned to stop fighting back a long time before then. I learned to lay in a ball to protect my face as much as possible and to avoid bruising. By doing so I was able to hide the abuse for years.

My daughters watched every bit of the brutal attack. Each time I attempted to stand to my feet he would knock me back down again. When I was finally able to stand on my feet, I ran to my bedroom and he was right behind me. He closed the door behind us and as I sat up against the wall I thought, it's finally over; but it wasn't. He began hitting me again but this time he kicked as well. Only two minutes had past but it seemed like forever.

I began questioning God as to why he allowed me to go through such a painful thing in front of my children. I wanted to know why, if He ordained the marriage, did it seem as though I was only experiencing heartache, pain, and suffering. Why had he forsaken me in this hour when I was living my best before him? I thought about my girls and said surely it would be better that I perish. I thought of myself as an embarrassment to my children, a disgrace, a coward. How cowardly of me to allow a man to put his hands on me in front of my children. Of all the prior abuse, I'd experienced, I only managed to call the police once but was unsuccessful with following through with the process and pressing charges.

I wondered who would raise my daughters. I knew I could not burden my parents with such a great responsibility. I knew there were alternatives but I did not want my daughters to be raised separately. I knew I couldn't lay on the floor and give up. I had a reason to fight and that reason was my daughters. I asked God to help me. My words were inaudible and short phrases. I'd say, "God help me. I need you. Strengthen me. Don't leave me."

The attack continued for a few more moments before I mustered up the strength to tell him if he didn't stop, I would call the police. This was a familiar phrase to him. I had spoken those words over and over again so they no longer held any power. Previously there had been no consequences attached to those words. To show me he didn't believe me he went and got my phone and handed it to me, daring me to call the police. I felt a demonic presence as he laughed and taunted me.

It was time for me to confront the devil. I had to show him I was not a coward and that he could not torment me any longer. I called 911 and explained what was happening and what had taken place. I gave the authorities his full name and informed them he had an active warrant for violation of probation.

Travis stared at me in amazement. He could not believe I had called the police and reported him. While on the phone with the operator he kept whispering to me to "hang up the phone." He repeatedly asked if I was serious and if I would actually proceed with it. I said yes over and over and over again. I felt more power each time I said yes. The operator advised that she would remain on the phone with me until the police arrived. When he saw I was not hanging up and that it wasn't a game, he left.

By the time officers arrived he was gone. I knew he could not have not gone too far because he left walking and we lived on the outskirts of the city, not close to anything within walking distance. Trying to find a ride at that hour was nearly impossible. The police observed the bruises on my face, neck and arms and took pictures. They asked if I wanted to go to the hospital and attempted to convince me to go but, because I did not want to disturb my parents at that time of the night, I declined.

The police informed me they would not be pressing charges against Travis. In that moment, my world came crashing down. I thought I'd have a nervous breakdown right there in front of the police officers. I asked them about the active warrant. Surely that alone should have been enough for them to pursue him and place him under arrest. They informed me they would go and search for him and they did.

As the officers searched the area, I felt some relief. I believed he would be captured and arrested. For the first time in months I felt as if I was starting to see the light at the end of the tunnel. I didn't call anyone to tell them what had happened while the police searched for Travis. I put things back in their places and cleaned up some of the mess that was made during the attack. I made sure the children were okay and put them to bed.

The police returned in what seemed like five minutes. I was happy to see them and assumed that Travis was in the back of their truck in handcuffs, but that wasn't the case. The police told me that they were unable to find him. I didn't believe they'd searched diligently and it left me feeling defeated. I felt as though my actions had warranted me no justice because the police had not protected me. I crawled into bed not knowing what my next steps would be.

Before I could fall asleep Travis returned. He knocked on the doors and when I did not answer he started knocking on the windows. He begged me through the windows to let him in. My phone chimed with text messages from him begging for forgiveness and requesting a second chance. Had I not been too sore to move, his request may have been granted. I didn't think there was any way to escape him. I couldn't stop him... neither could the police. I was revisited with thoughts of suicide but before I could contemplate them, one of my daughters came and crawled into bed with me. Her presence warmed my heart and I hoped again.

The next morning, I had a terrible migraine and was having trouble seeing. I knew I needed medical attention so I called my sister and asked if she would watch the girls for me so I could go to the emergency room. She told me she didn't mind. In response, I told her not to tell anyone I was going to the hospital.

Normally, she would have had suspicions about my request but the fact that she did not voice any concerns indicates to me that it was perhaps due to it being so early in the morning. She was probably still half asleep.

The girls and I loaded up in the car and headed to my parents' house, where my sister lived. I planned to arrive at my parents' house after they'd left for church. I didn't want to answer any questions about my visit or why I was leaving the children. When I arrived, I expected to walk in their garage because it was normally left open when they expected the girls and I.

I could only assume my sister had gone back to sleep so I rang the doorbell and was surprised when my step dad, Don answered the door. My mother had left for church already because she sang in the choir. Normally he was already at church too because he taught Sunday school.

He immediately directed his attention to my face and asked what happened. Without saying anything, a river of tears fell from my eyes. He summoned me to be quiet and asked me to look at him. He questioned whether or not I intended to return to the relationship. I shook my head to say no but in the back of my mind I questioned that answer. I knew leaving Travis was the right thing to do but it hadn't been the easiest thing to do. I let Don know I was going to the hospital and would return later to get the girls.

I left my parents' house and drove to the local hospital, checked myself in, and I let the nurses know what had taken place the night before. After I was checked into a room to be examined and treated, I climbed on the hospital bed and I laid on my back and stared at the bright light. I eventually drifted off to sleep; it didn't take much. I felt safe and at peace as I lay there. I had not rested that well in months.

I was awakened by moms' hand gently brushing my arm. When I opened my eyes, my mother was standing directly over me with tears in her eyes. Although she did not allow one tear to fall, I knew she was hurt. I knew the toxic relationship was starting to affect others. People I loved and people who loved me were affected; my children, friends, and family were all affected. I knew I could not return to the relationship.

While in the hospital, the nurses called the police; it was their legal obligation, because I had been in a domestic dispute. When I explained to the officer that previous authorities had not arrested Travis he was surprised. He explained to my mother and I that we could take out a warrant against him ourselves. He provided resources and directed me to local agencies which provided assistance for women who were victims of domestic abuse.

My immediate family assisted me with pressing charges against Travis and they helped me file for divorce. Both my immediate family and church family were financially, emotionally, and spiritually supportive throughout the process. I was finally free from the abusive marriage.

Although I was being abused, one of the reasons I didn't leave Travis during our marriage was because I was unsure of what God wanted me do. God is very clear concerning how he feels about divorce. As I searched scriptures, I couldn't find any to justify me divorcing Travis because of abuse. Let me pause to show you how God feels about violence through scripture.

Genesis 6:13 reads, "And God said unto Noah, the end of all flesh is come before me; for the earth is

filled with violence through them; and behold I will destroy them with the earth.

Here we see that God destroyed everyone on the earth because they were violent.

Jeremiah 22:3 says, thus saith the Lord; Execute ye judgement and righteousness, and deliver the spoiled out of the hand of the oppressor; and do no wrong, do no violence to the stranger, the fatherless, nor the widow, neither shed innocent blood in his place.

Psalms 11:5 The Lord trieth the righteous: but the wicked and him that loveth violence his soul hateth.

You need to understand that abuse is violence and God does not like it. At first, I didn't think I was a victim because it initially started as pushing. I compared my situation to other victims I'd heard about and I said things like, "oh, it's not that bad or he's not hitting me, and he does it because he loves me." Any form of violence is abuse and the situation will only get worse. In my case, the pushing turned into hitting, and escalated to biting and kicking. If you are experiencing any form of violence/abuse you are a victim.

I kept thinking that Travis would eventually change or that I would change him. I saw potential in him and I knew that he was better than his actions. The problem was that he did not see potential within himself. He didn't want to change neither did he want to become the person I was trying to make him become. People will only change when they want to change.

2 Corinthians 8:12 says, "For if there be first a willing mind, it is accepted according to that a man hath, and not according to that he hath not." This scripture indicates the first thing that is needed is a willing mind. My efforts to try and change him were pointless. There is liberty in Christ, which means he's not going to force anyone to do anything unwillingly.

I was the "ride or die" girlfriend and wife. I said phrases like, "I'll never leave you and I promise," which made me feel as though I was bound to the relationship. Those phrases made me feel that I owed Travis something I didn't. When I wanted to leave, because his actions didn't line up with his promises, he made me feel guilty. I lost cars, got evicted, lived in a state of poverty, and put my dreams on hold, waiting on someone to change who didn't want to change.

I tried to fight the battle alone by remaining quiet about my situation; I didn't open up to anyone. The devil used isolation as a wicked device. It wasn't until I opened up to my family members and church family that I was freed from the situation. Some battles are too great for you to try and fight on your own. God has strategically placed people around you to help you. I stayed in the relationship much longer than I should have because I tried to fight it alone.

When Travis' aunt made me feel guilty for calling the police, it was another form of isolation. The devil wanted me to think I was alone in my choice to call the police. Had I been in communication with people who gave me spiritual counsel their godly advice would have outweighed the one voice the devil used to make me think I was alone. If you are a victim of abuse connect with your immediate family and church family. Share your situation with them. Going to the abusers' family is not always the best idea. They may love you but they love him more. While they don't want to hurt you, their actions may be geared towards protecting him.

Don't be hindered by that one voice advising you not to get help. Make the abuser accountable for their actions. Do so by notifying the police and allowing them to be subject to the consequences of their actions. I hindered Travis for a long time without realizing it. I had the power to make him answer for his actions but by not doing anything my actions said I'm okay with you hitting me, nothing will happen to you if you do it again. Just as **Proverbs 3:12 tells us, God corrects those he loves,** we should correct the ones we love.

Call the police! I cannot stress this enough. You've already tried to change their behavior with your words and it didn't work. Your tears went unrecognized. Your actions will speak louder than your words. Call the police so that your abuser can learn from their mistakes and so you can find safety.

Your local police department can provide you with a variety of resources. There are safe houses and other organizations that provide legal aid to help you get a protection order. There are programs that provide financial assistance for domestic violence victims. Your local police department will have this information. You may believe you have a number of good reasons to stay with your abuser, but none of them outweigh your own safety and that of your children, if children are involved.

In case no one has told you, it's not your fault and you don't deserve it. You may be or have been victimized by phrases like, "you shouldn't have, it's your fault, or you got what you deserved." There is no truth in any of those phrases. Nothing justifies a man hitting a woman.

If you are in an abusive relationship and you are ready to be free, pray this prayer with me:

Dear God,

Thank you for life, health, and strength. Thank you that I am not sleeping in my grave. I thank you for protecting me while in the relationship that could have killed me. God, I ask you to open my eyes and cause me to see the situation the way that you see the situation. Provide an escape for me. Show me the people you have placed in my path to help me out of this situation. Show me the people you have placed in my life that I can confide in and trust for guidance and counsel. Lead me in your paths and give me direction in this situation. Send resources fitting for this situation. I ask that you give me the strength to leave this relationship and be not entangled again with the yoke of bondage. Sever every stronghold and every spiritual tie.

In the name of Jesus.

Amen

CHAPTER 7

Healing

The previous chapters reveal I had a pattern of leaving one bad relationship and entering into another. The root cause of my behavior was that I had not healed from my first relationship. For most of us, the first relationship we have is with our parents. Likewise, my relationship with my parents was my first and, though I was tremendously hurt in it, I never acknowledged my need to be healed.

To mask the pain from that relationship, I developed bad relationships with my peers. Their temporary acceptance and approval were like band-aids to my wounds. I joined gangs which gave me a sense of belonging; it was as if there were my family. Our loyalty was bonded by our words. I went to great extremes to please them for a continuance of their acceptance. When I was expelled from school and later incarcerated, I came to realized their loyalty was not equal to mine. I came to the realization that they only used me to do things they were too fearful of doing.

Hurt by unloyalty I experienced from peers I began engaging in promiscuity, drugs, and alcohol. I entered one bad relationship after another without giving myself time to heal in between those relationships. As I think back, I now realize, in each of those relationships, I was searching for the one thing I felt I'd lost in my very first relationship, family.

Let's take a look at *Mark 5:25-29*

25And a certain woman, which had an issue of blood twelve years,

26And had suffered many things of many physicians, and had spent all that she had, and was nothing bettered, but rather grew worse,

27When she heard of Jesus, came in the press behind, and touched his garment.

28For she said, If I may touch but his clothes, I shall be whole.

29And straightway the fountain of her blood was dried up; and she felt in her body that she was healed of that plague.

The first thing to be noted here, is that the woman realized she had an issue. It is important to first realize and acknowledge that you have an issue. After my divorce from Travis, I came to the realization that I had an issue. The same scripture goes on to tell us what the woman's issue was. Not only should you realize you have an issue, it is also important to know what that the issue is. The woman had her issue for twelve years. How far back does your issue go? Does your issue begin 15 years ago when your father left you? Does it begin 13 years ago when your mother was absent? If you don't know what the issue is ask God to show you. Ask the question, "God, what is my issue?"

The next thing we see is that the woman went from doctor to doctor looking for her healing. The bible goes on to say she **"spent all that she had."** I went from relationship to relationship, pouring out all I had. Each time I gave all of myself in hopes of being healed. I gave all of me in hopes of finding a family. As the scripture states of the woman, I did not get better. . . I only grew worse. Are you searching for a resolution to your issue in the wrong place? Is your current situation helping your issue or making it worse?

Verse 27 says *when she heard of Jesus. . .*
Romans 10:17 (AMP) says, *"so faith comes by hearing (what is said), and what is heard comes by the preaching of the message concerning Christ."* My

belief is that she was connected to a church body where she was being taught the word of God. It is important that you be connected to a church home where you are consistently hearing the word of God. Faith comes by hearing the word of God. She was able to complete the next part of the verse because she had faith.

Next, the scripture says, *"she came in the press behind."* Notice here that she only brought "her issue" before God. When you go before God bring no one else's issues but yours. I could not heal properly because I was going from relationship to relationship. God wants to heal us but it takes spending time with him. Who do you have in your life that is interfering with your process? This is an issue between you and God. Ask Him to remove the person or thing that is hindering you from being healed.

The next verse says, (paraphrasing) *"if I touch but the hem of his clothes, I shall be whole."* Speak your healing into the atmosphere. Declare that you will be whole. You will not be broken forever. Declare that your issue will touch Jesus and you will be healed. Make it your daily declaration until it manifests.

The last verse tells us, **the "fountain of her blood was dried up."** A fountain is an ornamental structure in a pool or lake from where one or more jets of water are pumped into the air. Imagine a lake or a pool. The fact that the writer uses the word fountain, I believe, indicates how massive the blood loss was. Yet, within seconds, God dried it up. My immediate thoughts are how great is our God! No matter how massive the issue is, it is not too big nor too hard for God!

The same scripture tells us, **"she felt her healing in her body."** The writer could have simply told us she was healed of the plague but he did not. My belief is that the writer wanted to demonstrate to us that our words have power. A couple of scriptures prior to that she was only speaking or voicing that she would be healed, but verses later she felt she had been healed. God has given you power and authority over every issue concerning your life. I declare that shortly after you speak your healing you will feel a change.

I also believe the writer used the phrase, **"she felt it in her body,"** because he wanted us to know the healing was done inwardly. God is going to heal you inwardly and it's going to manifest outwardly. Your life will never be the same, you will act differently, speak differently, you will love again, and you will allow others to love you. The visible signs of weakness and vulnerability will no longer exist. You will be healed!

CHAPTER 8
Dating Before Marriage

There were a few things I did not consider prior to my marriage to Travis. I would like to share those with you. It is my prayer that these will cause you to thoroughly think about your decision to marry. One of the challenges I faced was fact that Travis and I were unequally yoked. If you are walking with Christ, it is imperative that your husband is too.

Ephesians 5:22-25 says,

22 Wives, submit yourselves unto your own husbands, as unto the Lord.

23 For the husband is the head of the wife, even as Christ is the head of the church: and he is the savior of the body.

24 Therefore as the church is subject unto Christ, so let the wives be to their own husbands in everything.

First, you should desire a husband who is being led by God. The bible tells us, *"the husband is the head and the wife is to submit to him in everything."* Think about your head. The brain sends signals to the rest of your body and tells it how to function. If your brain is damaged it could possibly send wrong signals to other parts of the body or no signal at all. Because, Travis was not a believer so I thought I was exempt from being submissive.

Secondly, you should also desire a husband who seeks God when making decisions, for yourself, your children; even your finances. Also, consider the fact that you will be required to submit to the decisions made by your husband. *"The steps of a righteous man are ordered by God."* If God is not ordering your husbands' steps then who is?

Thirdly, you should desire a husband who is rooted and grounded in God. Even when you lose trust in your spouse you should be able to trust the God in him. I constantly found myself doubting Travis. We had many disputes because my relationship with Christ made him feel irrelevant.

I made decisions on my own thinking I was being led by God. "God told me to do this. God told me to go here." these were just a couple of examples of what I would say. His responses were, "Go ahead. You do what you want to do anyway." He felt as if his words carried no weight. I was in error and didn't realize it.

Continuing on the subject, believers have access to the gifts of the Spirit. We will discuss two of those here; discernment and conviction. Following disputes, I would pray and, at times, God would convict me and I would go apologize to Travis. Discernment gave me wisdom as to when and when not to speak. I chose my battles wisely. Every marriage has disagreements, but I can assure you when both spouses have the Holy Ghost it unlocks numerous gifts to help peacefully resolve issues that may arise.

The fourth thing I would like you to think about are the red flags. Can you live with those red flags for the rest of your life? I thought marriage would cause Travis to have a different outlook when it came to our relationship but I had to come to the realization that it would not. I thought it would mature him and make him more serious about our relationship. He had issues with faithfulness, staying at home, and maintaining employment. Those were red flags. They did not change overnight and they didn't change because we got married. Sometimes those "red flags" actually get worse. Marriage will not change the person you desire to marry.

Before we married, I'd always tell Travis to get out because of those red flags. I didn't consider the fact that those red flags would remain and I wouldn't be able to say "get out" anymore. I did not consider the fact that he would not change. Generally, you marry someone for who they are and because you love them. Not for who you want them to be.

⁶ And he said unto them, Is he well? And they said, He is well: and, behold, Rachel his daughter cometh with the sheep.

Genesis 29:6 (KJV)

¹⁰ And it came to pass, when Jacob saw Rachel the daughter of Laban his mother's brother, and the sheep of Laban his mother's brother, that Jacob went near, and rolled the stone from the well's mouth, and watered the flock of Laban his mother's brother.

¹¹ And Jacob kissed Rachel, and lifted up his voice, and wept.

¹² And Jacob told Rachel that he was her father's brother, and that he was Rebekah's son: and she ran and told her father.

¹³ And it came to pass, when Laban heard the tidings of Jacob his sister's son, that he ran to meet him, and embraced him, and kissed him, and brought him to his house. And he told Laban all these things.

14 And Laban said to him, surely, thou art my bone and my flesh. And he abode with him the space of a month.

15 And Laban said unto Jacob, because thou art my brother, shouldest thou therefore serve me for nought? tell me, what shall thy wages be?

16 And Laban had two daughters: the name of the elder was Leah, and the name of the younger was Rachel.

17 Leah was tender eyed; but Rachel was beautiful and well favoured.

18 And Jacob loved Rachel; and said, I will serve thee seven years for Rachel thy younger daughter.

19 And Laban said, it is better that I give her to thee, than that I should give her to another man: abide with me.

20 And Jacob served seven years for Rachel; and they seemed unto him but a few days, for the love he had to her.

Genesis 29:10-20 (KJV)

There are a few points I would like to discuss using the previous text. First, when Jacob saw Rachel, she wasn't idle; she was working! If you are preparing to marry you should be found working. While you should have something tangible to offer going into a marriage. You should also be working on the intangible assets you will ultimately bring to the table. In other words, you should be working on you.

A point to be noted is that Jacob also worked prior to marrying Rachel. A lot can be determined from an individual's work ethic. Jacob's commitment and faithfulness to his job says a lot about his character. The bible says, Laban was blessed because of Jacob. Jacob's work changed things around him. Consider your proposed husband. Does his work ethic provide opportunities for things to change for you? What does his employer say about him? What is said of his work ethic?

In verse ten Jacob saw Rachel and the sheep. He proceeded to roll the stone from the mouth of the well and watered the flock. Here, we can see Jacob's willingness. Prior to marriage Jacob was willing to help and assumed responsibility without being told to do so.

After meeting Jacob, Rachel went and told her father, who then came out to meet him. Allow your family to meet your significant other. Jacob wanted to marry Rachel first, but Laban (her father), said no that's not how we do things. Your parents can advise you of the right way to do things. If they have not been married or are not in your life someone else can give you godly advice about the right way to proceed. If you have no one in your family to turn to, go to your spiritual parents. You will need godly counsel when making major decisions like this.

After working seven years for Rachel, Jacob was still not allowed to marry her. He was told to wait. Verse 20 says, *"they seemed unto him but a few days, for the love he had for her."* *"For the love he had for her;"* it was because of his love for her that he was able to wait.

4Love endures with patience and serenity, love is kind and thoughtful, and is not jealous or envious; love does not brag and is not proud or arrogant.

5 It is not rude; it is not self-seeking, it is not provoked [nor overly sensitive and easily angered]; it does not take into account a wrong endured.

6 It does not rejoice at injustice, but rejoices with the truth [when right and truth prevail].

1 Corinthians 13:4-6 (KJV)

Require him wait for you. Save your virginity and require him to wait until after marriage before engaging in a sexual relationship. Make him wait until you complete the things God has assigned you to do in your singleness. There are some assignments God will only give you in your singleness. There are some ministries specifically designed for singles while others are designated for those who are married.

Don't be in a rush to marry. The man God has will wait and be available when you are ready to marry. Jacob was told to wait to marry Rachel. Take note: when it was time for them to marry Rachel wasn't found with anyone else, and Jacob's desire for her never changed. If he cannot wait, he's not the one God has for you.

CHAPTER 9
Generational Curses

Getting healed was only half of the victory for me. I also had to fight through generational curses. Although I wasn't raised by my biological mom, I didn't meet her until I was 18, I was on a similarly destructive path she had taken. My adoptive mother lived a holy and righteous life before me. The scripture promises us that if we, **"train up our children in the way they should go when they are old, they won't depart from it."**

Why had I departed? Why hadn't my sister, Jessica? She experienced the same divorce I did. Why hadn't she taken the same path I did? One answer, is that she chose not to respond to the situation in the same way I did. The other answer is that I was fighting generational curses that she did not have to fight.

You can have two people in the same situation with one fighting a different battle than the other. When Jesus was crucified, he wasn't crucified alone but with one person on his left side and another on his right side. Though their situations seemed similar, in that they were all being crucified, they each had different battles they were fighting. Just because someone is or has been in a situation you may have already come through doesn't necessarily mean you know everything they are battling with.

Because I was adopted, I don't believe my adoptive mom was fully aware of the generational curses I battled with. She was able to identify the issue and sometimes even be able to relate to the issue, but she didn't fully understand the underlying cause. Generational curses are brought on by the sins of our forefathers, going back to the 3rd, 4th and possibly the 10th generations.

Exodus 20:5 tells us, *"the consequences of sin are passed down from generation to generation."* We will look at the genealogy of David for an example of generational curses. David committed adultery and murder. Amnon, David's son committed incest with his sister Tamar. His brother Absalom killed him. Absalom slept with one of David concubines (2 Sam. 16:21-22), and he slept with ten more in public. Sexual immorality and murder are a couple of generational curses which were passed down.

Jesus, who's lineage is of the house of David, broke that curse for his family. If you are saved and have given your life to Christ, you are included in the family of Jesus. The curse has been broken for you and you have the power to break the generational curse for your family. To accomplish that, you must know what the curse is by identifying the spirits you are battling. Sexual immorality, alcoholism, smoking, addictions, lies, lust, anger, anxiety, depression, murder, pride, and profanities, are all examples of areas the enemy uses to establish generational curses.

Once you identify the generational curse ask God for deliverance. Connect with your pastor or someone in your church who is equipped to do deliverance ministry. Until this point, you have been in spiritual warfare but perhaps you did not realize it or know how to fight. To effectively fight against the devil, you will need the whole armour of God.

10 Finally, my brethren, be strong in the LORD, and in the power of his might.

11 Put on the whole armour of God, that ye may be able to stand against the wiles of the devil.

12 For we wrestle not against flesh and blood, but against principalities, against powers, against the rulers of the darkness of this world, against spiritual wickedness in high places.

13 Wherefore take unto you the whole armour of God, that ye may be able to withstand in the evil day, and having done all, to stand.

14 Stand therefore, having your loins girt about with truth, and having on the breastplate of righteousness;

15 And your feet shod with the preparation of the gospel of peace;

16 Above all, taking the shield of faith, wherewith ye shall be able to quench all the fiery darts of the wicked.

17 And take the helmet of salvation, and the sword of the Spirit, which is the word of God: 18Praying always with all prayer and supplication in the Spirit, and watching thereunto with all perseverance and supplication for all saints.

Ephesians 6: 10-18 (KJV)

The Armor of God are His garments which are not visible to us. They are used to fight against things the devil sends and uses against us. The curses we've previously discussed are examples of this. *Verse 10* tells us to, *"be strong in the Lord and in the power of His might."* Our strength and our might are not enough. That's why we need Gods strength, His might, and His garments.

Verse 14 tells us to, *"girt our loins with truth and put on the breastplate of righteousness."* Cover yourself God's truth. When the garment is removed the only thing that should be exposed is the truth. The breastplate of righteousness covers our heart and our soul. Our own righteousness is not enough. Paul declares in *Romans 3:10,* that *"there is none righteous, no not one."* Only God is righteous. His righteousness protects our heart and our soul.

The next verse tells us to, *"shod our feet with the gospel of peace."* Consider what shoes do. They allow us to walk freely without fear of stepping on something that could hurt us. To shod our feet with the gospel of peace is to walk with Christ freely, peaceably, and without fear, knowing we are safe in the comfort of His hands.

Verse 16 tells us to, *"take the shield of faith."* The shield of faith protects us from the darts of the enemy. One of the benefits of the metal shield Roman soldiers used is that is cannot be pierced. The shield of faith is what you believe. Your beliefs should not be quenched or pierced. The following are examples of darts the enemy may throw: you are ugly, you won't be anything, and you are worthless.

Your faith, what you believe, should resist those darts. Know that you are fearfully and wonderfully made. God made you to be somebody. You are valuable and should not be bothered by the darts enemy throws. Choose to believe what God says about you.

Verse 17 says, *"put on the helmet of salvation and take the sword of the spirit."* The helmet protects us against blows to the head. It protects our minds from ungodly thoughts sent by the enemy. It doesn't allow the enemy to plant seeds of negativity in our minds. The sword of the spirit is the word of God. Find scriptures about your situation and meditate on them. Fill yourself with the word of God daily.

Lastly, *verse 18* tells us to, *"pray always."* When you are in warfare, cover yourself in prayer on a daily basis and spend time praying in the spirit. Once your behavior changes and you are delivered, don't turn back! You can break the curse off yourself but returning to sin can reinforce it. Once the curse is broken off your life, you also break it of those in your family living under you. Continue to do so by living holy and righteous before them; being mindful to continually pray over them.

Here is a prayer for breaking generational curses. Personalize this prayer by saying the name of the curse(s) you have identified:

Dear God,

I repent and ask that you forgive me of my sins. The sins that I do willing and the sins that I do unwilling. Lord I ask that you break every generational curse in the name of Jesus. I command every unclean spirit and every spirit that is not from you to come out in the name of Jesus. I command all dormant spirits to come out in the name of Jesus. God help me to put on the whole armour of God that I may be able to withstand the fiery darts of the enemy. Teach me how to fight against the enemy.

In the name of Jesus, I pray.

Amen

CHAPTER 10
Redeemed

Earlier, I shared that my biological mom delivered me while a prisoner of the state. Because she was a prisoner of the state there was some delay in identifying who would raise me. During the majority of my teenage years and young adult life, I was ruled by state probations and confined to jail cells. I was owned by the state. Sin ruled me and I too considered myself to be a prisoner of the state.

Have you ever had to bond someone out of jail or have you ever had to be bonded out of jail? The cost for making bond can be quite expensive. Regardless of the cost, or a persons' guilt or innocence we can safely say that one is often bonded out by their loved ones. You may not have bonded anyone out of jail, but have you ever paid a price to fix someone else's mistake because you love them?

Jesus bonded me out! That is my testimony. It didn't matter how deep of trouble I was in, whether I was guilty or innocent, right or wrong. Jesus bonded me out! The price He paid for my bond was his life. I was bought with a price and you were too. When I gave my life to Christ I was redeemed and God completely turned my life around.

The word redeem means to, "compensate for the faults or bad aspects of something." When I say God redeemed me, I also mean He turned around every bad place and every place of pain in my life and made it work together for my good. The devil meant for my parents' divorce to destroy me. Both my adoptive parents remarried. My biological mom also got married and turned her life around. I now have 3 sets of parents, all of whom are active in my life and in the lives of my children. The devil meant for my parents' divorce to kill the person God called me to be before I could even realize who I was, but I have been redeemed!!!

You too can be redeemed and used by God. You were bought with a price, now go, glorify God in your body and in your spirit because you belong to Him. YOU ARE REDEEMED!

www.ingramcontent.com/pod-product-compliance
Lightning Source LLC
Chambersburg PA
CBHW061957040426
42447CB00010B/1797